See how they grow
Rabbits

Kathryn Walker

WAYLAND

First published in 2007
by Wayland

Copyright © Wayland 2007

Wayland
338 Euston Road
London NW1 3BH

Wayland Australia
Hachette Children's Books
Level 17/207 Kent Street
Sydney, NSW 2000

British Library Cataloguing in Publication Data
Walker, Kathryn, 1957-
        Rabbit. - (See how they grow)
        1. Rabbits - Juvenile literature
        I. Title
        636.9'32

ISBN 13: 978 0 7502 5255 3

Printed in China

Wayland is a division of Hachette Children's Books,
an Hachette Livre UK company.

The publishers would like to thank the following for allowing us to reproduce their pictures in this book:

Getty images: cover (Martin Ruegner /Image Bank), title page and 19 (GK Hart/Vikki Hart/Image Bank), 11 (Steve Shott/Dorling Kindersley collection), 17 (Gary Randall/Taxi), 18 (Catherine Ledner/Stone), 22 (Wendy Ashton/Taxi). Discovery Picture Library: 9, 23. FLPA: 4 (David Hosking), 5 (Gerard Lacz), 6 (Cyril Ruoso/JH Editorial/Minden Pictures), 7 (Edwin Giesbers/Foto Natura), 8 (Foto Natura), 13 (Andrew Parkinson), 14 (Nigel Cattlin), 15 (Gerard Lacz), 20 and 21 (Mike Lane). Istockphoto: 10, 12 (Barbara Henry), 16 (Nico Smith).

Contents

What is a rabbit?

Rabbits are found in many parts of the world. Wild rabbits live in woods, grasslands and sand dunes. They are like **domestic rabbits** in many ways. Domestic rabbits are ones that people keep as pets.

▼ Strong back legs and feet help a rabbit to move quickly.

Rabbits have very good hearing. Their eyes can see in almost all directions. Their twitching noses quickly pick up new smells. Rabbits are always looking out for signs of danger. Many animals kill rabbits for food.

▲ A rabbit's large ears can turn in any direction to pick up a noise.

Wild rabbits

Most types of wild rabbits live in large groups. They live together in **warrens**. A warren is a set of underground holes, or **burrows**. Narrow tunnels link these burrows together.

▼ Rabbits shelter inside their warrens.

Rabbits sleep in their burrows for most of the day. They leave their burrows to find food. They usually do this in the evening and early morning.

▲ These rabbits are keeping watch at an entrance to their warren. Each warren has several entrances.

7

Domestic rabbits

More than 2,000 years ago, the ancient Romans farmed rabbits for meat and fur. Today lots of people keep rabbits as pets. Rabbits enjoy the company of people.

▲ Rabbits often get on well with other family pets, such as guinea pigs.

Rabbit Fact

You can train a rabbit to use a litter tray. This is important if the rabbit is kept indoors.

Regular brushing helps to keep a pet rabbit clean and healthy.

A rabbit is born

A mother rabbit can have between four and twelve babies at a time. Rabbit babies are called **kittens** or kits. The mother prepares a cosy nest for her kittens. She pulls fur from her own body to make this nest.

▼ Kittens' eyes stay shut for the first few weeks of their lives.

The kittens are born without fur. At first they cannot hear or see. The mother visits her nest once or twice a day. Then the kittens can feed on her milk.

▶ The mother's milk gives her kittens all the food they need for the first few weeks.

Growing up

At three weeks the kittens' eyes are open and they have thick fur coats. They begin to eat solid food. Rabbits finish growing when they are between six and eight months old. Female rabbits are called **does** and males are called **bucks**.

▲ Kittens huddle together when they are tired. This helps them stay warm.

Rabbit Fact

Pet rabbits can live for eight to twelve years. Many wild rabbits die in their first year.

▼ Young rabbits like to explore, but they stay close together for safety.

What rabbits eat

Rabbits eat only plants. Wild rabbits eat grasses, roots and berries. Pet rabbits need vegetables, fruit and hay. They should also have special rabbit food from a pet shop.

▼ Rabbits like to eat crops, like the barley in this field. This is why farmers see them as pests.

▼ Rabbits like to gnaw on wood. This stops their teeth from growing too long.

All sorts of rabbits

There are many different types of rabbit.
The type that you see in the wild are
usually grey-brown in colour.

Rabbit Fact

Hares are members
of the rabbit family.
Hares are bigger than
rabbits. They have
longer legs and ears.

◀ Unlike rabbits,
most hares prefer
to live alone.

Pet rabbits come in all sizes and colours. There are special types called **breeds**. Some breeds have long hair. Some have long, floppy ears. These are called lop-eared rabbits.

▼ Lop-eared rabbits look cute, but they cannot hear as well as other rabbits.

17

Choosing a pet rabbit

You need to choose a pet rabbit carefully. Some types grow to be large and will need big **hutches**. Long-haired rabbits need lots of brushing to stop their coats from getting tangled.

◀ This breed of rabbit is called the English Lop. These rabbits can weigh more than 5 kg. All rabbits must be picked up very carefully, as this boy is doing.

▼ Pet rabbits are happier when they have company.

Rabbit Fact

Most rabbits do not like being picked up. They need to be handled gently as they can easily be injured.

Pet rabbits like to have a companion. It is best to have two female or two male rabbits from the same **litter**.

Making a home

A pet rabbit needs a hutch with two parts.
The main part should have a wire mesh door.
This is the living space. The other part should
have a solid wooden door and **straw** inside.
This is where the rabbit sleeps.

A rabbit hutch needs to be cleaned out every day.

A rabbit needs to run about outside its hutch. A long wire cage in the garden is the best place. This is called a **run**.

▼ A rabbit can eat fresh grass and wander about safely in a run.

Caring for a rabbit

A pet rabbit will need regular food and plenty of hay to eat. You need to clean out its hutch every day and make sure it gets plenty of exercise.

Playing helps a rabbit to stay fit and happy. Boxes, balls and tubes all make great toys.

▼ Rabbits can make great pets if they are carefully looked after.

▼ Big tubes like this can be play tunnels. They are a bit like a burrow and make good places to rest.

Glossary

bedding
Material used to make a comfortable place for a rabbit to sit or sleep. It may be a mixture of newspaper and wood shavings, straw and hay.

breed
A special type of rabbit.

buck
A male rabbit.

burrow
A hole in the ground made by a rabbit. It is used as a place to shelter.

doe
A female rabbit.

domestic rabbit
A rabbit that is kept as a pet.

hay
Cut and dried grass used as food for some animals, such as rabbits.

hutch
A cage for small animals, such as rabbits. A rabbit hutch is usually made of wood and wire mesh.

kitten
A baby rabbit.

litter
The offspring, or young, born to an animal at one time.

litter tray
A tray that an animal uses as its toilet.

run
A long cage that protects rabbits as they wander about outdoors.

straw
Dried stems of plants such as wheat or barley. It is used for animals to sleep on.

warren
A set of underground holes and connecting tunnels where rabbits live.

Index